# CHARITIES IN ACTION

# SAVING THE ENVIRONMENT

*Andrew Langley*

**www.raintreepublishers.co.uk**
Visit our website to find out
more information about
Raintree books.

**To order:**
☎ Phone 0845 6044371
🖷 Fax +44 (0) 1865 312263
🖳 Email myorders@raintreepublishers.co.uk

Customers from outside the UK please telephone +44 1865 312262

Raintree is an imprint of Capstone Global Library
Limited, a company incorporated in England and
Wales having its registered office at 7 Pilgrim Street,
London, EC4V 6LB – Registered company number:
6695582

Text © Capstone Global Library Limited 2012
First published in hardback in 2012
The moral rights of the proprietor have been
asserted.

Edited by Andrew Farrow, Adam Miller, and
    Diyan Leake
Designed by Victoria Allen
Picture research by Ruth Blair
Illustrations by Oxford Designers & Illustrators
Production by Victoria Fitzgerald
Originated by Capstone Global Library Ltd
Printed and bound in China by Leo Paper
    Products Ltd

ISBN 978 1 406 23849 5 (hardback)
16 15 14 13 12
10 9 8 7 6 5 4 3 2 1

**British Library Cataloguing in Publication Data**
Langley, Andrew.
Saving the environment. -- (Charities in action)
363.7'057632-dc23
A full catalogue record for this book is available from
the British Library.

**Acknowledgements**
The author and publisher are grateful to the following
for permission to reproduce copyright material:
Alamy pp. 17 (© Tryphosa Ho), 29 (© Mark Conlin), 33
(© Penny Tweedie), 34 (© Keith Morris), 39 (© Lana
Rastro), 41 (© AF archive); Bush Heritage Australia
p. 49 (© Peter Morris); Corbis pp. 9 (© Robert Van
Der Berge/Sygma), 11 (© Phil Klein), 13 (© Narendra
Shrestha/epa), 21 (© Greenpeace/epa), 25 (© Ralph
Clevenger), 31 (© Andrew Lichtenstein), 45 (© Noel
Hendrickson/Blend Images), 51 (© David Brabyn),
52 (© Jiang Fan/Xinhua Press), 55 (© Tim Pannell),
57 (© Alain Felix/Hemis); Earthwatch p. 47 (Simon
Wallace); © Friends of the Earth International p. 5;
courtesy of Fundación ProAves (www.proaves.org)
p. 19; Getty Images pp. 27 (Sion Touhig), 37 (Robert
Harding World Imagery/Michael Runkel); © Dave
Lauridsen p. 22; The Wilderness Society p. 43.

Cover photograph of divers collecting octocorals for
the Queensland Museum collection as part of the
Coral Life census, Lizard Island, Queensland, Australia,
April 2008, reproduced with permission of Naturepl
(© Jurgen Freund).

Every effort has been made to contact copyright
holders of material reproduced in this book. Any
omissions will be rectified in subsequent printings
if notice is given to the publisher.

# CONTENTS

Words printed in **bold** are explained in the glossary.

# WORLD IN DANGER

Our environment is under threat. **Icecaps** are melting, seas are rising, and the climate is changing. Drought, earthquakes, and storms are becoming more frequent. Fuel is running out, and water and air are being polluted. Many animal and plant species are disappearing. Can we do anything to stop this process? Thousands of people who work for environmental charities all over the world believe we can.

## People and pollution – Caroline's story

Caroline Ntaopane is a volunteer. She works for a charity near Johannesburg in South Africa. Its aim is to make sure that people in the local community are treated fairly over the **pollution** of their environment by major industries.

Caroline has to face environmental problems every day. She lives just 100 metres (328 feet) from a giant chemical plant in the Vaal region. She sees the smoke filling the sky and the roar of the flares burning waste gas. She feels the machines shaking the ground under her feet, and smells the stench of the chemicals. Many neighbours, including members of her own family, have breathing problems due to the pollution.

In 2005, Caroline helped launch the Vaal Environment Justice Alliance (VEJA). This represents local environmental groups, who work together to tackle the damage caused by chemical and steel companies in the area. For many years, waste from their plants has been polluting air and water sources, and the government has done little to regulate them.

The VEJA measures air and water quality in the area, **monitors** how waste is managed, and checks the health of local people and company workers. Caroline oversees the monitoring, organizes meetings, and publicizes the work of the charity. There is not enough money to pay someone to run the office, so she does most of the paperwork as well.

## Working for change

What inspired Caroline to volunteer for an environmental charity? The turning point came in 2002 when she visited the United States. Here she saw how pollution affects everyone – but those who suffer most harm are usually poor, black, and disadvantaged. This is especially true in parts of South Africa, where many black people live in poverty. "I really want to see change happen," she says, "and I have the experience, passion, and capabilities to help bring about that change." Sometimes it feels as if they are struggling against huge obstacles and getting nowhere. "But I know we are making a difference."

There are many thousands of people like Caroline Ntaopane all over the world, who have dedicated themselves to doing something positive about the massive problems facing our environment. Some have full-time jobs with environmental charities or other **non-profit organizations**. Others work for free in their spare time. You will meet many of them throughout this book.

Caroline Ntaopane campaigns for better air quality for all in the Vaal region of South Africa.

# What are the major threats to the environment?

The world's **ecosystems** are being damaged in many ways. Most of these ways are connected. Scientists agree that human activity is the main cause of the damage. Here are some of the biggest threats.

• *Climate change*:  Earth's atmosphere is getting warmer, due partly to a build up of **carbon** gases. This causes icecaps to melt, leading to a rise in sea levels.

• *The energy crisis*:  **Fossil fuels** (such as coal and petroleum) will soon run out. New and sustainable forms of generating energy will have to be developed.

• *Pollution*:  Modern society produces chemicals and waste that poison soil, air, and water. Industry and agriculture are among the biggest polluters.

• *Population growth*:  The world's population is growing faster every year. We need to produce more food and other essentials, and cope with more waste.

• *Disappearing farmland*:  Climate change, pollution, and other factors are degrading large areas of land. These can no longer be used for growing food.

## Governments and greenness

Who can solve these problems, which endanger the future of life on this planet? One answer is international agencies such as the United Nations (UN), which can reach all corners of the world. This organization runs a massive project called the United Nations Environment Programme (UNEP), which helps developing countries to protect their environments.

Many national governments work to combat threats to the environment. But they find it difficult to agree with other governments about how to deal with the threats. They are also under pressure from industrial and business leaders not to take actions that might harm the **economy**.

Most developed countries have their own agencies devoted to green and conservation issues. In the United States, there is the Environmental Protection Agency (EPA), which enforces rules on matters such as air and water quality. The United Kingdom has the Department for Environment, Food, and Rural Affairs (DEFRA).

## Getting warmer

In its 2007 report, the global agency Intergovernmental Panel on Climate Change (IPCC) showed how dramatically Earth's atmosphere is hotting up. For example:

- the period 1995–2006 contained 11 of the hottest 12 years since records began;
- between 1993 and 2003, sea levels rose by an average of 3.1 millimetres (0.12 inch) a year;
- the area of ice in the Arctic is shrinking by an average of 2.7 per cent each decade.

Different environments all over the world are under threat. This map shows some of the areas studied in this book, as well as places where research is going on to find solutions.

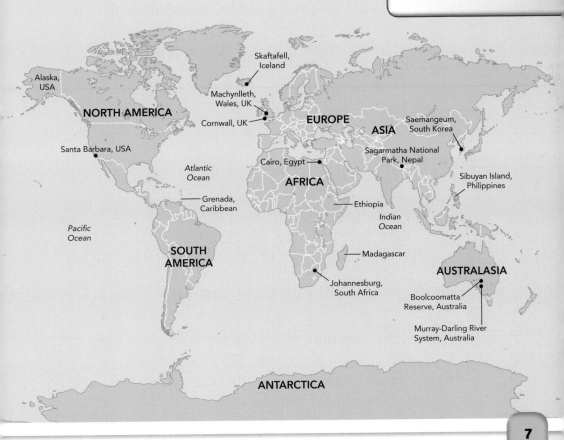

Skaftafell, Iceland

Alaska, USA

Machynlleth, Wales, UK

NORTH AMERICA

Cornwall, UK

EUROPE

ASIA

Saemangeum, South Korea

Santa Barbara, USA

Atlantic Ocean

Cairo, Egypt

Sagarmatha National Park, Nepal

AFRICA

Sibuyan Island, Philippines

Grenada, Caribbean

Ethiopia

Indian Ocean

Pacific Ocean

SOUTH AMERICA

Madagascar

AUSTRALASIA

Johannesburg, South Africa

Boolcoomatta Reserve, Australia

Murray-Darling River System, Australia

ANTARCTICA

## Charities make a difference

Charities have a very special role to play in dealing with environmental problems. There are several hundred charities throughout the world devoted to tackling a wide range of green issues. Every one is created and run by people who are genuinely committed to making the world a greener place. They are funded by donations from individuals, corporations, and governments.

What makes charities different? For a start, they are usually private and independent (unlike most politicians), and are not influenced by governments or big businesses. They are also not-for-profit organizations, which means that they do not have to give surplus wealth to shareholders. Instead, they use it to carry out their programmes.

## Global and local

Some of the larger environmental charities, such as Friends of the Earth or ActionAid, are global bodies. They operate in many parts of the world and are involved in many different types of activity. Charities like this are well known through advertising and news stories, and draw enormous sums in donations each year.

Many other charities are less famous and work on a smaller scale. Some, such as the Chesapeake Bay Foundation in the United States, are concerned with the conservation of a specific area. Others are focused on a single kind of activity, such as promoting **solar energy**, planting trees, or protecting a specific animal species or **habitat**.

## What do charities do?

Environmental charities do not all work in the same way. There is a huge variety of methods for achieving their specific aims. Among these are:

• *Practical help*: giving assistance to those people who are worst affected by pollution, energy shortages, or the many problems caused by climate change;

• *Education*: informing and alerting the public about threats to the environment, their impact on our lives, and how they can be dealt with;

• *Conservation*: restoring and protecting habitats that have suffered damage;

• *Direct action*: challenging and obstructing projects which may pose serious dangers to people and ecosystems.

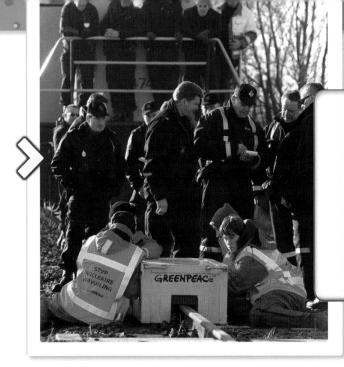

Greenpeace activists chained themselves to railway tracks to disrupt the transport of nuclear waste. The yellow box is difficult to remove, and it delayed the train by one hour.

## Different ways to help the planet: Dateline June 2011

**1.** "GLOBAL CHARITY'S GOAL TO PLANT ONE MILLION TREES"

With this headline, the Plant a Tree Today Foundation (PATT) launched an ambitious plan. The charity aims to plant one million new trees in Thailand, Indonesia, and other Asian countries. These will restore forests which have been cut down, not only helping local people but also fighting against climate change caused by the loss of native habitats.

At one end of the process is Runrueng Lengwilas, who runs the plant nursery in Sap Tai, Thailand, where thousands of new trees are grown. He is also an experienced nature guide. At the other end are the bands of PATT staff and volunteers who clear scrub and actually plant the trees.

**2.** "GREENPEACE BLOCK NUCLEAR WASTE TRANSPORT"

**Activists** from the charity Greenpeace International made a dramatic protest against **nuclear energy** in The Netherlands. Ten Greenpeace volunteers chained themselves to the railway track in order to stop a train carrying **radioactive** waste materials for processing in France.

Which kind of action against environmental threats do you think is more effective? How dramatic do anti-nuclear protests have to be to get noticed?

# PLANNING FOR ACTION

Starting up an environmental charity is a huge challenge. Keeping it going, and making it successful and effective over a long period, is even tougher. The challenge is even bigger at times of global economic hardship, when people and governments have less money to donate to good causes.

## Setting up

What are the most important things needed to plan and launch a new charity?

• *A clear vision:* The founders have to know exactly what their values and aims are, and have a realistic plan of action for achieving them.

• *Lots of research*: Are there charities out there already doing the same sort of work for the environment? There's no point in simply duplicating campaigns – it could damage established organizations as well as the new one.

• *The right staff:* Volunteers and other staff have to be dedicated to the goals of the charity, prepared to work hard, and enthusiastic about what they do.

• *Funds up front:* It should be able to pay staff and set up programmes as soon as possible. This means surviving without donations at first, because many people are unwilling to give money to an organization with no track record.

• *Getting the paperwork done:* Most countries have strict rules about how charities should be founded and run. They have to have a written set of rules, called a constitution, and a board of trustees, a group of people who oversee the charity's work.

## Carrying on

To steer a charity through good and bad years demands enthusiasm and passion. But, like any other business, it must also be run professionally. Managers have to be familiar with regulations concerning non-profit organizations. They should make regular reviews of progress, to make sure they are sticking to their original vision.

Charities aim to explain clearly what they are doing. So they publish regular reports about their activities, research findings, education programmes, and publicity campaigns. They also have daily office work to do, including recruiting and training staff, ordering materials, and keeping in contact with people working in the field.

## Making a living

Charities deal with other people's money, so they have to manage their finances carefully. Donations should be used in the most efficient way. How much should be spent on fieldwork, and how much on advertising? How much should staff be paid? Charity workers generally earn less than most people, but still need a living wage.

On top of this, the charity has to live within its means. Setting a realistic **budget** for spending each year, and sticking to it, is vital. Detailed accounts must also be kept of money coming in and going out.

### How many charities?

*The number of charities throughout the world is mind-boggling. There are at least 1.1 million in the United States alone, of which over 300 are involved in green issues. In the United Kingdom, there are 168,000 charities in all. At least 100 of these are environmental.*

Demonstrators carry signs against Diablo Canyon Power Plant during the Mothers for Peace Nuke Protest in Avila Beach, California, USA, in April 2011.

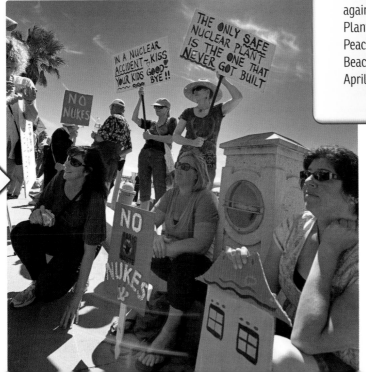

# Friends of the Earth International

Friends of the Earth International (FoEI) is the biggest environmental network of them all. It campaigns on a huge variety of urgent environmental and social issues all over the world. It is also one of the oldest green organizations, having celebrated its 40th birthday in 2011.

## How is the network organized?

FoEI is not just one charity, but a vast group of them, covering every continent and 76 countries. Its members include over 5,000 local activist groups, and it has more than 2 million members and supporters. The network is supported by its headquarter's office in Amsterdam in The Netherlands.

## The main targets for FoEI

• *Agrofuels*:  Energy companies are grabbing land in less developed countries to grow fuel crops instead of food. FoEI educates people about the dangers of this, and urges financial institutions to stop supporting the agrofuels sector.

• *Climate justice and energy*:  The world faces **global warming** and an energy crisis due to wasteful fuel use by some countries. FoEI works for the right of all people to have an equal share in energy resources.

• *Food sovereignty*:  FoEI believes people should be able to control their own food systems. It supports small peasant farmers against the power of big corporations, which often destroy their livelihoods.

• *Forests and **biodiversity***: The world's forests are being destroyed to provide timber, farmland, and other products. Member groups work with local communities to manage forest resources, and campaign against exploitation.

• *Resisting mining*: The search for fossil fuels causes many environmental disasters. FoEI groups support communities damaged by this and challenge governments to find alternative and **sustainable energy** sources.

## FoEI in action

FoEI members take part in many hundreds of environmental campaigns all over the world. A few examples are listed on the opposite page.

### Australia

The Murray–Darling River system in Victoria is drying up, thanks to climate change and water extraction. Activist groups are campaigning to save it. They want the government to buy back water licences from farmers and other water users.

### Nepal

Melting glaciers threaten the famous Everest (Sagarmatha) National Park. FoE Nepal has helped draw up a petition to protect the area. It was supported by climber Sir Edmund Hillary (one of the first people to climb Everest, the world's highest peak) and conservationist Sir David Attenborough.

### South Korea

FoE Korea and other groups are pressurizing the government to halt a land reclamation scheme on the Saemangeum tidal flats. This is destroying a beautiful part of Korea's coastline and an important **wetland** ecosystem.

### Uganda

A Ugandan environmental organization is working to stop mining companies from illegally quarrying limestone and drilling for oil in protected areas such as national parks and the Rift Valley.

One of the greatest environmental threats to Nepal is caused by global warming. This has melted snow high in the Himalayas, which swells mountain lakes and increases the threat of serious flooding.

## Green workers

Big or small, local or global, a charity needs skilled staff to run it. At the top are the directors or trustees. These people are independent and unpaid but usually experts in the kind of work the charity does. They make the big decisions about the group's campaigns and finances. These decisions are put into effect by the chief executive officer, who is in charge of the daily running of the organization.

The rest of the workforce is usually divided into two parts. One includes all the people who work in the field, either overseas or locally. They may do a huge variety of tasks, from running projects to collecting information.

The second part includes the administrative staff. They support the field workers, raise funds, control the finances, and run the charity's offices.

## What skills are needed?

People want to work for an environmental charity because they are committed to its causes. But good charity workers need more than passion and enthusiasm. They will have to work with others, and make their own decisions. So they should be reliable, sensible, and self-confident. They should also be self-motivated and good at communicating and organizing.

## Being an intern

Some green charities take on young people for periods of work experience, which are usually unpaid. These are called internships. An **intern** is generally a university or college graduate, or in some cases a high-school student, with a real interest in environmental matters.

An internship can last from two or three months to an entire year. In that time, the intern may take part in a job that will help him or her to develop personal skills and learn about how a charity works. Areas of work for interns include event planning, public relations, plant raising, regional conservation, **archives**, and even looking after a children's zoo.

## Conserving traditional communities

In 2011, Jennifer Hanlon was an intern for the Alaska
Conservation Foundation in the far northern United States.
Her internship lasted for 12 weeks of the summer, during
which she gathered information about the culture of the
area. Jennifer was born and raised in Alaska, growing
up in a traditional hunting community where people
still live off the land. So she is interested in the way our
natural environment defines how we live. She believes that
ecosystems have to be healthy to support people living
in close harmony with the land.

## How a big global charity works

A big charity, such as Conservation International, works on a large
number of projects worldwide. To do this effectively, it needs a large
workforce (400 at headquarters, and nearly 600 in the field). It also
needs a strong structure. This diagram shows the staffing structure
of Conservation International:

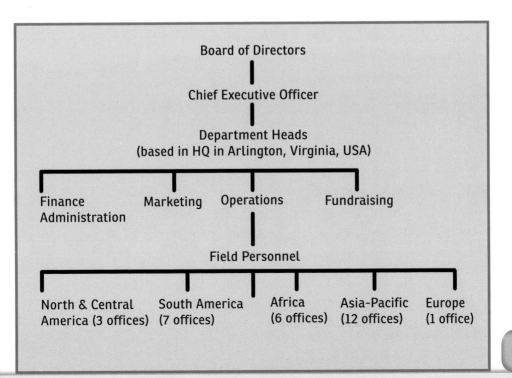

Board of Directors

Chief Executive Officer

Department Heads
(based in HQ in Arlington, Virginia, USA)

Finance | Marketing | Operations | Fundraising
Administration

Field Personnel

North & Central | South America | Africa | Asia-Pacific | Europe
America (3 offices) | (7 offices) | (6 offices) | (12 offices) | (1 office)

# GOING GLOBAL

The best-known environmental charities are usually the biggest ones, such as Greenpeace, ActionAid, or WWF. Their publicity campaigns and appeals are seen all over the world, and raise vast amounts of money each year. This is spent on big projects in most parts of the developing world. They employ hundreds of people and have offices in major cities.

## Across the planet

The large charities have many ways of working – giving practical help, giving financial or expert support, campaigning, or just raising public awareness. Here are some examples of big organizations using their money and knowledge to help provide solutions to major environmental problems.

### Global warming

*What's the problem?* The world is getting hotter, due largely to the build-up of carbons in the atmosphere.

*Who's tackling it?* The Rainforest Alliance works to preserve the huge forest ecosystems in tropical areas, which act as natural storage organs for carbon, thus keeping it out of the atmosphere. The Alliance supports farmers and companies who use rainforest products in a sustainable way.

### Sustainable farming

*What's the problem?* Many modern farming practices damage the environment, causing land **degradation** and pollution.

*Who's tackling it?* The Soil Association, based in the United Kingdom, has been promoting greener ways of farming. These include the use of organic fertilizers, the reform of intensive systems such as caged poultry, and closer ties between farmers and their communities.

### Alternative energy sources

*What's the problem?* The world needs to find renewable sources of energy to replace fossil and nuclear fuels.

*Who's tackling it?* The Wilderness Society in the United States has backed a massive solar power project on the Crescent Dunes area of Nevada. This will help the state to generate more electricity while lowering its **emissions** of carbon (from burning fossil fuels).

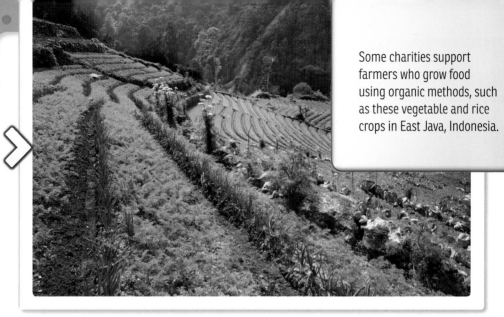

Some charities support farmers who grow food using organic methods, such as these vegetable and rice crops in East Java, Indonesia.

## Damaged ecosystems

*What's the problem?* The world's fragile ecosystems are being damaged or destroyed by climate change, natural disasters, and other threats.

*Who's tackling it?* Wetlands International works to preserve and restore the wetland areas of the world. One of its projects is helping local communities in Aceh, Indonesia, to replant their mangrove forest ecosystem.

### Aldo Leopold (1887–1948), Pioneering US conservationist and ecologist

As a young man, Leopold worked for the Forest Service in Arizona and New Mexico. One of his duties was to shoot predators such as bears and mountain lions. He soon learned to respect the place of such animals in their environment, and went on to recommend the preserving of wildlife habitats in the United States. In 1935, he was one of the founders of the Wilderness Society, pledging to protect the country's wilderness areas. His book *A Sand County Almanac* became a bestseller after his death. He stated that:

"We abuse land because we regard it as a commodity belonging to us. When we see land as a community to which we belong, we may begin to use it with love and respect."

17

# The World Land Trust: Securing the rainforests

The rainforests of Latin America are disappearing fast. Logging, mining, and agriculture destroy vast areas every year. How can they be saved? The obvious answer is to buy them. This is the aim of the World Land Trust (WLT), based in the United States and the United Kingdom. Since 1989, the charity has raised enough money to purchase over 680,000 hectares (1.7 million acres) of endangered forest – an area bigger than the Irish Republic. This keeps it safe – forever.

Sir David Attenborough, who is Patron of the World Land Trust UK, says: "You will not save endangered species unless you save the whole ecosystem. And to save an ecosystem you need to save the land. That is what WLT's project partners do."

## Buy an acre

The WLT has a simple offer to make. One acre of threatened land costs, on average, £100. Anyone who donates this sum has saved an acre of rainforest. Smaller donations from individuals, and much larger ones from businesses and other organizations, are also collected to purchase land in vulnerable areas from private owners.

The charity works very efficiently. Of the money it raises, only about 3 per cent is spent on administration. This means that over 96 per cent goes towards buying and helping to preserve as much rainforest as possible.

## Partners in the project

The WLT does not buy large chunks of rainforest directly. It works through local conservation groups, which negotiate the deals with the owners. The charity selects these partners carefully to make sure they have the right motives, skills, and experience.

The WLT provides the money to pay for the land. But once the land has been secured, it does not belong to the charity. It is owned by the local partner groups, who manage the site and are responsible for protecting it. The WLT gives them support and expert advice about conservation and research. Such deals depend on one thing: money. Without enough donations, the WLT would not be able to buy anything, or train people to protect the sites.

## What's been saved?

Since it was founded in 1989, the WLT has raised enough money to preserve vital rainforest habitats, including:

- *Peru*: reserves which protect communities of **indigenous** Amazonian peoples;
- *Bolivia*: a giant nature reserve protecting some of the world's most endangered species of birds;
- *Ecuador*: unique "cloud" forests high in the Andes;
- *Chile*: an ecosystem which contains some of the world's oldest trees;
- *Venezuela*: 16,000 hectares (40,000 acres) of forest and grassland.

Paul Salaman of WLT with children in the community of Puerto Pinzón, a village in Boyacá, Colombia.

### Dr Paul Salaman: the Trust's Director of Conservation

At the age of eight, Paul met the famous broadcaster and natural history writer (and later WLT patron) Sir David Attenborough. This meeting inspired him to become a naturalist and conservationist. At age 14, he was already managing a small nature reserve in London. As a student, he led expeditions across Colombia, finding several birds new to science. He helped found the El Dorado Nature Reserve there, which he calls "the ultimate Noah's Ark, protecting the last populations of many critically endangered flora and fauna; a living treasure trove like no other on Earth". Paul has worked for the World Land Trust US since 2008.

## Same goal – different methods

The buying of threatened land is an effective scheme for saving threatened rainforest areas. But this is just one method of campaigning to save our environment. There are many global green charities, and they have many different ways of achieving their aims. Some give practical help to prevent damage. Some raise money to repair damage that is already done. Others take direct action to protest against people they see as environmental villains.

## Two ways of fighting the fuel crisis

### Direct confrontation

On 17 June 2011, activists from Greenpeace International landed on an oil-drilling platform operated by Cairn Energy off the Arctic coast of Greenland. As the activists climbed the 30-metre (98-foot) ladder, rig crew tried to drive them back with sprays of freezing water. When they reached the platform, the activists were arrested.

Why did Greenpeace do it? Their leader, Kumi Naidoo, said, "Because Arctic oil drilling is one of the defining environmental battles of our age. The rapidly melting cap of Arctic sea ice is a grave warning to all of us, so it's madness that companies like Cairn see it as a chance to drill for the fossil fuels that got us into this climate change mess in the first place. We have to say, 'No more'." The protesters were later released without charge.

This is an example of direct action that confronts businesses that may be causing environmental damage. Greenpeace's aims were to disrupt the drilling and create a dramatic news story that would be seen and read all over the world. This gains publicity and helps put pressure on governments who allow oil exploration in vulnerable areas such as the Arctic.

### Practical help

How can poor people in **less economically developed countries** get access to cheap and sustainable energy sources? In March 2009, the Global Village Energy Partnership (GVEP International) launched a unique competition in South America and the Caribbean. Local and international businesses were challenged to think up ideas for increasing the supply of renewable, low-cost energy in the region. Here are some of the winning ideas.

- Turning waste from locally produced foods such as cheese, coffee, and bananas, into ethanol, which can be burned to generate heat and power
- Producing gas and liquid fuel by processing old vehicle tyres

- Making low-cost solar water heaters from recycled materials
- Developing special **turbines** to generate electricity from slow-moving rivers
- Enabling shrimp fishermen to use nightlights powered by the Sun, instead of gas or oil
- Inventing a system that finds the best sites for generating power from tidal currents.

Winners were given grants of £12,500 over two years to develop their schemes.

This is an example of giving practical help to the people who need it most. The ideas make little use of harmful fossil fuels, and do not need huge plants or power stations to produce the power.

## Protest and the law

*Every country has its own laws about demonstrations and other disruptive actions. Anyone who stages protests may be acting illegally, depending on where they are. Even though their actions are non-violent and cause no damage, protestors may end up in jail. They must be prepared to accept the consequences for what they do.*

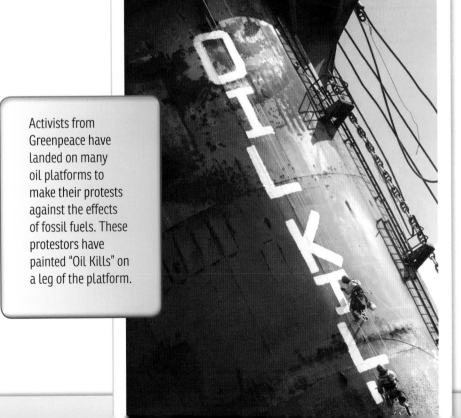

Activists from Greenpeace have landed on many oil platforms to make their protests against the effects of fossil fuels. These protestors have painted "Oil Kills" on a leg of the platform.

# Making a difference

Global charities do a huge amount of work in protecting our planet and its people who are under threat from pollution, climate change, and other dangers. Without them, the world's environment would be in an even worse mess than it already is. But green organizations can also make a huge difference to the lives of the people who work for them.

## Homeless and hopeless

When he was 15 years old, Joshua Carrera and his family were evicted from their apartment. They had to live in a shelter in Brooklyn, New York City, USA, for nearly a year. Life was hard, and Joshua was unsure about how he would get away from the shelter, at least for the summer. "I was angry," he says. "I was confused and lost. Of all my friends, I never thought I would be the one homeless." Then he heard about a programme run by the Nature Conservancy charity. Called Leaders in Environmental Action for the Future (LEAF), it offered paid internships on conservation projects for students from poor and urban areas.

Joshua applied for a place on the programme, but was rejected. He was devastated. The next year he applied again and this time was accepted as an intern. That summer he headed for the Lake Champlain valley in Vermont. It was an experience that would change his life.

An internship with the Nature Conservancy helped Joshua Carrera to change his life. He now does fieldwork and other research in threatened areas of North and South America.

## Out in the wilds

Like most LEAF students, Joshua knew nothing about life outdoors in the countryside. He had rarely ever been out of the city. "Everything I knew about nature was from documentaries and the Discovery Channel," he recalled. Now, suddenly, he had to get used to long, hard days of work in the open air.

His job was finding and clearing weeds that were choking the nature reserves run by the Conservancy in Vermont. Joshua had never worked so hard in his life. "Coming from New York City, I always had the freshest pair of kicks on, I always cared about the way I dressed," he says. "Working in nature meant dressing differently and not caring about getting your hands dirty."

He also found that he enjoyed the peace and the challenges of the job, from canoeing on lakes to hiking long distances with a heavy pack. He learned self-reliance – budgeting his money, and washing his clothes. Most important of all, he found a sense of purpose he had never had before.

## A career in conservation

Joshua's experiences that summer convinced him that he wanted to work with nature. He landed other internships with the Conservancy in North America. He started other charity projects of his own, such as raising money to build homes for indigenous peoples in Guatemala. He has done fieldwork research in Ecuador (where his family is from).

### The Nature Conservancy

Founded in 1951, the Nature Conservancy is one of the oldest and biggest environmental charities. Its aim is to preserve the diversity of life on Earth by protecting plants, animals, and ecosystems. Based in the United States, the Conservancy has projects in more than 30 countries around the world. These include grasslands in Kenya, freshwater habitats in China, and coral reefs in the western Pacific.

# COMMUNITY CONSERVATION

There are several hundred big global charities devoted to the environment. However, the number of local, small-scale green organizations runs into several thousands. In fact, no one knows exactly how many there are all over the world. These bodies usually focus on issues that directly affect their community, such as cleaner public transport, or pollution from power stations, or threatened habitats in the area.

## Small can be beautiful

Of course, local charities do not have the influence, the wide news coverage, or the money that big organizations enjoy. They have small staff numbers, and many of these work for little or no pay. They can rarely afford massive publicity campaigns or offer many internships.

However, the smaller groups do have many advantages. By choosing a single issue, they can concentrate their attention on it completely, and are often able to exert a lot of pressure on governments or corporations. By tackling environmental problems that affect the immediate community, they can appeal directly to local people. These people may not usually get involved with charity work, but are more likely to support campaigns on their doorstep.

## Fighting for the local environment

How can communities get inspired to act on local green issues? Often it needs a lot of hard work from environmental groups in the area to enthuse and inform people. This means not just highlighting the problems posed by pollution, global warming, habitat destruction, or other threats. The groups also have to offer practical solutions, and show how they can be made to work.

Some areas of the world have especially active community groups. In the US state of California, for example, dozens of local green organizations are campaigning for their own towns or departments to lessen their harmful impact on the environment.

Among these is the Community Environment Council (CEC) in Santa Barbara. Its major project, called "Fossil Free by '33", aims to encourage local people to stop the use of all fossil fuels in the region within a generation (by 2033). They believe this can be achieved through:

- the use of electric cars;
- solar, wind, and wave energy;
- building new, more efficient housing;
- only buying products with a low **carbon footprint**;
- centring communities round people, not cars.

### Green energy: Megan Birney

*Megan Birney is part of the team running the Santa Barbara CEC. She specializes in renewable energy. She provides information to local people and business owners who want to invest in renewable sources (such as solar power), and helps the CEC support local energy projects. She gives advice to local governments about how to tackle climate change and **greenhouse gas** emissions. Megan also finds time to teach a course on renewable energy at the local university.*

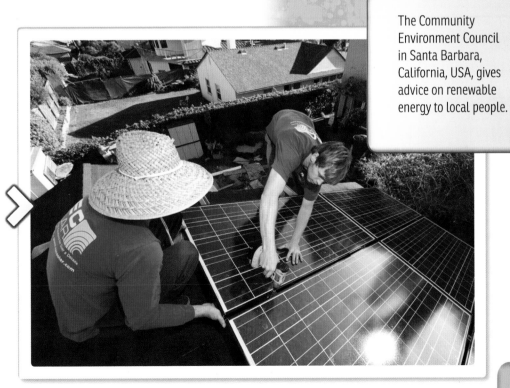

The Community Environment Council in Santa Barbara, California, USA, gives advice on renewable energy to local people.

## Action in focus

Smaller charities can concentrate their full attention on a single area or problem. Despite their size, their enormous range of activities can have a powerful effect on a wide variety of environmental threats. Here are some examples of how local or special-interest organizations are tackling two of today's major green issues.

## Preserving the landscape

*Irish Peatland Conservation Council:* The bogs (wetland areas) of northern Europe are a unique ecosystem. They not only provide a habitat for flowers and animals, but also a natural storehouse for carbon and a record of past cultures and climates. For centuries, the Irish have cut peat (compacted vegetable matter) from the bogs, which was dried and burnt as fuel. The IPCC protects a sample of unspoilt peatlands across Ireland, repairing damage and educating people about their importance. The Council has just seven full-time staff.

*Sibuyanons Against Mining:* Sibuyan is one of the most beautiful and unspoilt islands in the Philippines. Since 2006, it has been threatened with extensive mining for nickel, gold, and other valuable materials. SAM has been at the forefront of opposing the mining applications from Australian and other companies, which endangered nearly half the island. It has organized petitions and mass rallies, and gained support from governments and environmental charities all over the world.

## Preventing pollution

*Surfers Against Sewage (SAS):* SAS was formed in Cornwall in 1990 by surfers who were made ill by seawater polluted with sewage. Its mission was to publicize and protest against the pumping of raw sewage and other toxic waste into the sea. Since then, SAS has pressurized water companies into treating their sewage. It has also tackled the problems of beach litter and dangerous pollution from shipping.

*Association for the Protection of the Environment (Egypt):* The huge Egyptian capital of Cairo produces a vast amount of garbage. Much of this is gathered for free and then sorted and recycled by the people of the Mokattam area. The APE fights for the rights of these amazingly efficient rubbish collectors, who recycle up to 90 per cent of what they collect. The charity runs projects to improve working conditions, and to make their work safer and easier – as well as providing schools and healthcare.

Members of Surfers Against Sewage staged a "toilet protest" in Brighton. This highlighted the way raw sewage is pumped directly into the oceans.

### The Big Green Bus

Every summer, the Big Green Bus travels all over the United States, from Mississippi through California and Wyoming and up to New Hampshire. On board are Dartmouth College students, whose mission is to encourage Americans to help create a sustainable future. At each stop, they give information and useful tips about renewable energy, how to cut their carbon emissions, and other environmental matters. The bus itself has been converted into an educational exhibit. It has solar panels, rechargeable batteries, and bamboo floors – and its engine runs on recycled cooking oil.

# Sandwatch – caring for the world's beaches

Grenada has some of the most beautiful beaches in the Caribbean. In the summer of 2010, these were invaded by hundreds of school students. Armed with measuring tapes, microscopes, water testing kits, and bin bags, they spread out over the sands and set to work. They cleared up rubbish, measured wave heights and currents, tested water quality, and made maps of beach **erosion** and vegetation.

Altogether, students from twelve Grenadian schools took part in this project. They planned to come back at least once a month to repeat their measuring and clearing. In this way, they would be able to keep watch on how the beaches altered over time, through erosion, pollution, and other forces.

## Global – and local

Grenada's project is part of a much bigger campaign to monitor and protect the world's beach environments, called Sandwatch. This is not a single organization, but a network of small, local, action groups in many islands and coastal areas, covering more than 40 countries. These stretch from the Pacific islands and South America, across Europe and Africa all the way to eastern Asia.

Sandwatch is a true grassroots movement. It was launched in 1999 by the United Nations Educational, Scientific, and Cultural Organization (UNESCO) as a volunteer network of school students, teachers, members of youth groups, and other community bodies. Its aim is to make young people aware of the fragile nature of the coastal environment, and of the vital need to use it wisely.

## How are beaches monitored?

Here are the main measurements and other activities that Sandwatch volunteers need to complete on a field trip:

- sketch map of beach
- beach erosion/**accretion** (high-water mark, taken at three places from fixed points with photos)
- beach composition (samples of sand for microscope/magnifying glass. Note materials, colour, size, and texture of grains)
- human activity on beach (make notes and photos of types and numbers)

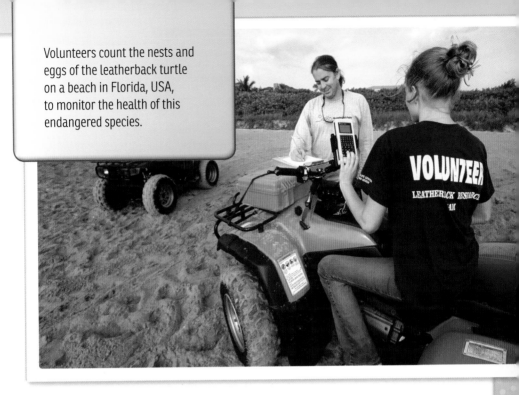

Volunteers count the nests and eggs of the leatherback turtle on a beach in Florida, USA, to monitor the health of this endangered species.

- beach debris (clean beach and note types, with photos)
- wave characteristics (height, frequency, direction, water, and air temperatures)
- measure current (use dye markers to measure how much dye moves over 60 seconds from a fixed point in the water)
- flora/fauna (note types of animals and plants on and around beach)
- test water (nitrate, phosphates, salt, and other chemical levels)

The Sandwatch project achieves a lot in conserving the world's beaches and coastal seas. But it also has other valuable benefits for local communities.

- It educates young people about the threats to the coastal environment and the importance of sustainable development;
- It reinforces school work in other related areas of the curriculum, such as science and mathematics;
- It encourages school students and other community members to learn and work together;
- It empowers ordinary people to have a real and positive impact on the world around them.

## Getting together

Environmental groups have many different aims and programmes. But they are heading in the same general direction. They all want to make the world a healthier and fairer place, and to protect its environments and people from the likely disasters produced by climate change.

The smaller charities and non-profit organizations sometimes find it hard to get their messages heard. However, if they work together on similar or related projects, they can make a stronger impact. This works especially well for local groups, who can take part in wide-ranging campaigns to make their communities, cities, or counties greener.

## Making it local

This can also work the other way round – with a national organization running local trusts and charities. Groundwork USA, for example, is a collection of community-based partnerships in cities all over the country. These include Dallas, Denver, Milwaukee, New Orleans, Portland, and San Diego. Advice and organization come from its headquarters in New York City.

The trusts work to regenerate and improve their environments in many ways. They reclaim vacant or derelict land for conservation or recreation areas. They clean up polluted brownfield (old industrial) sites and make them healthy and usable again. They encourage local businesses to support non-profit groups.

Amongst Groundwork's recent achievements are:

- clearing a factory site in Minneapolis so it can be used as a park and wetland reserve;
- cleaning rubbish and undergrowth that was choking part of the Saw Mill River, a tributary of the Hudson River;
- helping schools build and maintain gardens in San Diego;
- introducing an energy-efficiency programme to households in Denver;
- helping to construct a green trail through the centre of Gary, Indiana.

Volunteers plant a garden on an industrial site on the banks of the Gowanus Canal in Brooklyn, USA. The area was targeted by the US government's programme to clean up the nation's uncontrolled hazardous waste sites.

## A day in the life...

What is it like working as a conservation volunteer at a local charity, far from home? Here is a typical day of volunteer Jenn Beard, who worked for the Azafady Conservation Campaign out in the bush in Madagascar during 2010.

Dawn: Woken by the Sun rising and one of the cooks banging a spoon on a pot of rice. Other days we might be treated to dough balls or banana bread. After breakfast we fetch water from the well and get to washing up.

7.30 a.m.: Out into the bush to measure and study specimens of trees or lemurs, search for reptiles, build beehives, help to restore drains, clear weeds, or teach at the school.

12.00 midday: Back to camp for lunch of rice and beans, and a rest during the hottest part of the day.

2.00 p.m.: A lesson in the Malagasy language with one of the guides. We learn about simple conversations, buying goods, and how to count and tell the time.

3.00 p.m.: Back to work – either continuing from the morning or doing something else entirely.

Sunset: Return to camp to finish anything daylight is needed for and have dinner. After dinner dishes are done we talk, play games, laugh, or just look at the stars.

# EDUCATING FOR CHANGE

The most obvious work of many charities is the practical help they give. Raising money for equipment or restoring habitats is vitally important. But education is just as important – especially for organizations that are devoted to green issues. Most environmental action bodies see educating and informing as the first step in protecting endangered parts of the world.

## Why educate?

Green charities have three main targets for their educational work. The first is the vast number of people in the front line who are directly affected by climate change or pollution. These include farmers, forest workers, and threatened indigenous peoples who can be given special training to help them deal with the results of environmental changes – for example, water shortages or increased flooding.

The second target is the world of industry and business. Mining and manufacturing companies, for example, have been responsible for a vast amount of carbon emissions and pollution of air, soil, and water supplies. Charities and other pressure groups have engaged with large and small companies, and helped them find ways of lessening their harmful impact on the environment.

The third target is the general public. Many of the growing threats to our environment do not seem dramatically obvious. They do not hit the headlines, in the way that terrible famines, droughts, or earthquake disasters do. So it is vital to inform and alert people about the dangers facing the planet from "invisible" factors, such as global warming or the crisis in energy supplies.

## Learning about the environment

Education also plays a major part in the structure of many green charities and other non-profit organizations. Many staff members (especially those in the field) have studied environmental subjects at school and university. The charities often prefer to employ people who have gained degrees or other qualifications from their courses.

There are two major areas of learning. Environmental Science examines how the Earth and its systems work. It is based on the sciences, including physics, chemistry, and biology, as well as ecology (plant and animal relationships) and geology. Environmental Studies examines how humans interact with their environment.

## Send a Cow – save lives

Amsalu Haile is a farmer in one of the most remote areas of Ethiopia in Africa. Ten years ago, his ten children were always hungry. But then he got help from the charity Send a Cow, which trains families in natural farming methods that are kind to the environment. It also provides them with the seeds, animals, and tools they need. With Send a Cow's aid, Amsalu started to grow more food. He can now afford to pay for his children to go to school. He also works to pass on his new knowledge to help others, and has trained more than 20 neighbouring farmers.

Sylvie was left an orphan after civil war in Rwanda, and looks after her brothers and sisters. She was given a goat to provide vital milk by the Send a Cow charity.

## Catch them young

Many charities have recognized the crucial importance of educating children about green issues. Young people who are aware of the problems threatening our planet will be better equipped to solve them in the future. For example, WWF has been helping to educate children in the United Kingdom about the environment by running a "One Planet Schools" programme. This offers resources, activities, and tools for teachers and students. It helps them to get in touch with other schools around the world, share information, and coordinate lesson projects.

In the United States, the Conservation Fund is heading a campaign to reconnect children with the natural world by getting them outdoors. Called "Outdoor Nation", it sponsors clubs all over the country where kids can enjoy camping, hiking, mountain biking, gardening, and other activities.

### Education

*"The most important task, if we are to save the Earth, is to educate."*
Peter Scott (1909–1989), ornithologist and founder of WWF

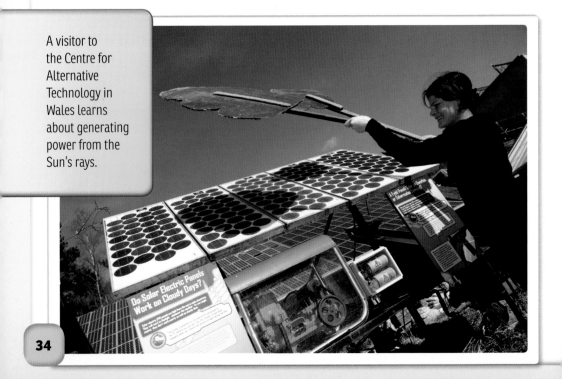

A visitor to the Centre for Alternative Technology in Wales learns about generating power from the Sun's rays.

# Changing attitudes: greener living

How can an environmental disaster be avoided? Most pressure groups believe that humans will have to alter the way they live. Everyone will need to make big changes, such as using renewable energy sources, building more efficient homes, and learning to recycle waste. To do this, they need to be taught about new attitudes and skills.

Some charities are devoted almost entirely to educating ordinary people in this way. The Centre for Alternative Technology (CAT) near Machynlleth in Wales runs courses in all aspects of green living, from organic food growing and woodland management to eco-sewage (toilet waste) systems and rainwater storage. Visitors can see examples of renewable energy in action, including wind turbines, solar panels, and water-powered generators.

## Sustainable buildings at CAT

Emma Donnelly joined the 2011 Architecture Summer School run by the Centre for Alternative Technology. The aim of the course was to teach students about designing and constructing buildings using sustainable materials and methods. One project was to build a stand for the Shambala Festival. She says:

"It's now half-way through the summer school, and Day 1 of building a festival structure for Shambala by the end of the month. There are 10 of us in the team, plus two tutors. Day 1 has been great. After our team briefing, we set about measuring, sawing, screwing, chiselling, and carrying our components. The structure is three timber-frame 'petals' 3.5, 4.2, and 5.5 metres [11, 14, and 18 feet] high. We started with the middle-sized petal. And that was pretty big! I can't wait to see the whole thing!"

## The Sierra Club

The Sierra Club, founded in California, USA, in 1892, is one of the world's oldest environmental groups. Its original mission was to protect the Sierra Nevada region. Today the club has thousands of members throughout the United States. Its educational programmes aim to attract people of all generations, cultures, and abilities, and to teach them how to protect the environment. The Sierra Club's education centre is in Yosemite, the famous national park and World Heritage Site.

# The power of the Sun: Solar Energy International

A lot of people understand that we cannot go on using fossil fuels. Many also know about the importance of harnessing the natural energy of the Sun, wind, and water to generate power instead. But very few can actually install a solar panel or build a wind turbine, let alone make use of the electricity they produce.

Solar Energy International (SEI) was created to train people in those skills. It is a non-profit organization that encourages people to learn the practical side of renewable energy resources. Based in the US state of Colorado, it educates and instructs people from all over the world about how to install and maintain sustainable systems of generating power. These include solar **photo-voltaic cells** (PVCs), and wind and water turbines.

## What does SEI do?

• *Courses and workshops in the United States*
Over the past 20 years more than 16,000 people from all 50 states and 66 other countries have attended SEI's renewable energy courses. The organization's team of instructors has trained them to design, construct, install, connect, and maintain solar and other systems.

• *Online training*
Many of these courses can be taken online by students overseas. They have also been translated into Spanish to cater for the huge number of students from South American countries.

• *Women's courses*
To encourage more women to gain skills in renewable energy, the SEI runs special sessions that are run by women for women.

• *Native American courses*
The SEI works with Native American environmental groups to run courses and provide installations for reservations. The aim is to help Native Americans build new energy networks.

• *Solar in the Schools*
Children are taught the basics of renewable energy through classroom presentations by SEI instructors, while their teachers can attend workshop courses.

- *Business services*

The SEI creates courses specially suited to individual companies. It also gives help to other non-profit organizations.

- *International programmes*

Over 2 billion people in less developed countries of the world have no access to modern forms of energy. The SEI has run training courses and workshops for groups in nations across the globe, from Mexico and Ecuador, through South Africa and Palestine to Pakistan and the Solomon Islands.

Solar panels can be fitted anywhere which gets a lots of sunlight, such as this traditional house in the Sahara Desert region of Algeria.

## Hugh Piggott, wind turbine wizard

Hugh Piggott is SEI's expert on wind generators and works as a training instructor on workshop courses. He has been working with wind power for over 30 years, and has built many turbines – the biggest was nearly 5 metres (15 feet) in diameter. Hugh has also designed small wind turbines for use in Zimbabwe, Sri Lanka, and Peru.

"I dream about wind machines all the time. We live in a world rich in free, natural energy, which is out there for the taking. There are few thrills to beat a well-engineered wind turbine working in a good breeze."

Hugh Piggott

# MONEY AND PUBLICITY

Without money, charities and other non-profit organizations would not exist. They need a constant supply of funds to pay for their projects, their offices and staff, and their fundraising operations. At the same time, charities need publicity. It is vital that as many people as possible know about their aims and campaigns. This will bring them support – and donations.

## Sources of money

Have you ever put money in an environmental charity worker's tin? Or donated online during a national television campaign? These are the most obvious ways of raising cash to save the planet. But donations are just one of several sources which keep charities afloat.

• *Donations from individuals*:  These are made by ordinary people passing collectors in the street, through major appeals in the media, or through sums of money left in someone's will (after they die).

• *Donations from businesses*:  Many companies and corporations give regular sums to charities. Some even match the donations made by their employees.

• *Donations from charitable trusts*:  Anyone who wants to set aside some of their wealth for charitable causes can set up a trust. These trusts will give money to selected charities.

• *Government grants*:  National governments and international bodies (such as the UN) pay regular sums to certain charities.

• *Tax relief*:  Most people and businesses have to pay taxes on the money they earn. However, many governments give charities freedom from these taxes.

• *Charity earnings*:  A charity can earn income in many ways – through selling goods they have produced (such as books), or by selling services (such as technical training or advice).

## How do charities spend their money?

Environmental charities raise their cash from public and private sources. By law, they have to account very strictly for how they spend it. Here are the figures for some big organizations mentioned in this book. It shows the percentages of their incomes they spent on their projects (practical work in the field), on administration (running the office and paying staff), and on fundraising and promotion (publicity and campaigns).

**Where charities spend their money (in percentages)**

| Charity | Projects | Administration | Fundraising | Other |
|---|---|---|---|---|
| Conservation Fund | 97.2 | 1.7 | 0.9 | 0.2 |
| Earthwatch Institute | 83.4 | 10.3 | 6.1 | 0.2 |
| Friends of the Earth | 85.5 | 7.5 | 6.8 | 0.2 |
| Nature Conservancy | 77.9 | 13.0 | 9.1 | N/A |
| Rainforest Alliance | 94.1 | 0.8 | 4.9 | 0.2 |
| World Land Trust | 96.5 | 2.6 | 0.8 | 0.1 |
| WWF | 77.2 | 0.1 | 14.6 | 0.1 |

If you look closely at the table, you can see that some charities spend much more on administration or fundraising than others. Why do you think this is? Remember that bodies such as the WWF conduct a lot of publicity and press campaigns that put pressure on governments and corporations. They also encourage individuals to act – not just to donate money, but to spread news, sign petitions, and demand changes. Most of the others do not do this, so their spending patterns are different.

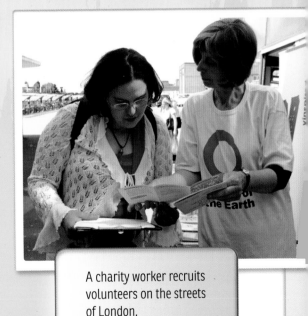

A charity worker recruits volunteers on the streets of London.

# Al Gore and the Alliance for Climate Protection

One of the biggest charity success stories in recent years has been the growth of a new organization, the Alliance for Climate Protection (ACP). Surprisingly, it grew out of a failure. In 2000, Al Gore lost the race to become the US president. After this, he devoted much of his time to publicizing the problems of climate change.

Most famously, Gore starred in the 2006 documentary film called *An Inconvenient Truth*. This used factual evidence to argue that climate change was caused by human activity, and would lead to catastrophe if we did not change our way of life. The film became one of the most successful documentaries of all time. That same year, Gore founded the Alliance for Climate Protection.

## What does the ACP do?

The ACP is not a practical charity aimed at directly helping people affected by environmental issues. It is all about publicity and **lobbying**. Its mission is to discover and call attention to the shocking reality of the climate crisis. By using modern communications (through Facebook, Twitter, and other social networking sites), it has been able to carry its message swiftly across the world.

These are the Alliance's major projects:

*The Climate Project*
The ACP has a worldwide force of lecturers who educate people about the looming crisis of climate change, and the ways to fight it. Their main campaign tool is a slide-show version of the facts from *An Inconvenient Truth*.

*Repower America*
This campaign calls for the United States to switch to a cleaner energy system, with more efficient energy use, power generated from renewable sources, and investment in electric cars.

*The We Campaign*
Launched in 2008, this urged Americans to pressurize their government into making major reductions in carbon emissions.

*The Climate Reality Coalition*

In September 2011, the ACP teamed up with the Sierra Club and other green bodies for a worldwide live, streamed event. Its aim was to expose the full scale of the climate crisis.

## Are celebrities good for charities?

There are many non-profit groups who campaign on climate change. So why has the ACP had such a rapid growth, and gained so much publicity? This is partly due to the work of its staff and supporters. But the biggest reason is the fact that Al Gore is famous, powerful, and wealthy. He was even awarded the 2007 Nobel Peace prize for his environmental work.

Is this a good thing for the environmental movement as a whole? The ACP is certainly using enormous amounts of money in its projects. In 2008, it announced it would spend $300 million (£188 million) on its global We Campaign. The sum was raised thanks to Gore's contacts, and the success of his books and film. Is this money that could have been given to other charities? Would the cash have been better spent on more practical projects? What do you think?

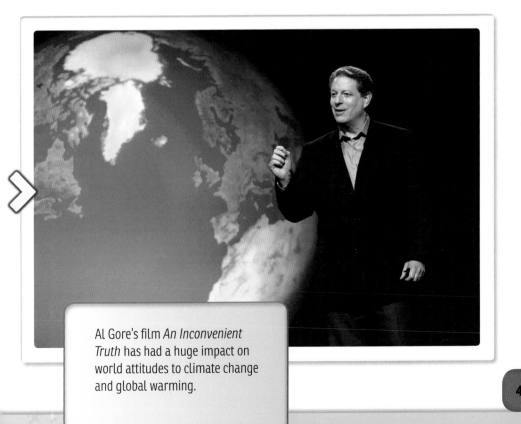

Al Gore's film *An Inconvenient Truth* has had a huge impact on world attitudes to climate change and global warming.

## Getting noticed

For their work to have an impact, green charities need publicity almost as much as money. They have to get their message across clearly to as many people as possible. The message might be asking for donations or new members, or drawing attention to threats to our environment. Persuasive and powerful publicity is the best way to encourage support and help the organization achieve its aims.

So media campaigns are an important part of charity work. Most large non-profit groups have an expert team devoted to this, with large budgets to pay for national advertising and other mass publicity. Smaller charities have less money to spend, so they have to focus their media messages on specific groups or areas.

## Using the media

There is an enormous variety of news and advertising media, from newspapers and magazines to radio, TV, and social networking websites. Publicity and press officers for charities have to choose carefully the most effective ways of employing them. How much will it cost? How many readers or viewers will it reach? Is its audience likely to be interested in the message?

Basically, publicity comes in two forms:

• *Free*: Newspapers and broadcast media are always looking for a good newsworthy story that is fresh, interesting, and unusual. Many green issues provide such stories, whether it is Greenpeace activists protesting on an oil-drilling platform or Send a Cow training farmers in Ethiopia. The charity's press officer sends out details of the story in a **press release**. If journalists are interested, they will follow it up, either in a feature article or a recorded interview. Publicity of this kind is free.

• *Paid for*: Charities can also buy publicity. They can pay for posters or magazine or TV advertisements. They can mail leaflets, advertising material, and donation forms to millions of households. They can send emails and messages through mobile phone texts and social network sites. And they can keep their own members informed about events through newsletters and their own websites.

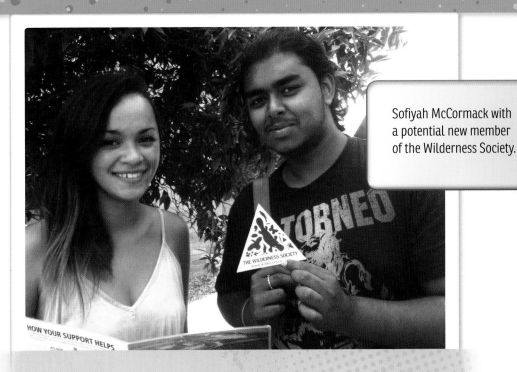

Sofiyah McCormack with a potential new member of the Wilderness Society.

### Sofiyah McCormack, Wilderness Defender Campaigner

The Wilderness Society in Australia works to protect and preserve the country's wild places, plants, and animals.

Sofiyah is a Wilderness Defender. Her job is to go out and meet members of the public, tell them about the organization, and encourage them to become members. Sofiyah says the most rewarding part of her work is "helping people remember how powerful we all are, and that each of us is more than capable of creating a better world".

Working for the Wilderness Society has taught Sofiyah a lot. Besides fundraising techniques, she says she has learned "resilience, patience, and compassion. I've also met some pretty amazing people that I might otherwise have never crossed paths with." Sofiyah has had the opportunity to travel all over Australia as part of her job.

Recruiting new members brings in most of the organization's money, so the work of fundraisers like Sofiyah is vital in helping to run publicity campaigns and carry out conservation work. Sofiyah knows how important her job is – she is helping to protect beautiful places, and is proud to make a difference as part of an **ethical** organization.

# RESEARCH

Advances in technology and science have made a huge impact on our lives. They have also helped cause a lot of damage to our planet over the past 200 years. For example, new machines, chemicals, and factory processes have brought pollution and global warming. But technology may also hold the solutions to these problems by developing cleaner and more sustainable ways of living.

## What is research for?

To cope with or prevent environmental disaster, we have to learn more about the Earth and how we affect it. Researchers provide crucial information to help with this crisis. Their work covers most green issues, such as:

• *Habitat conservation*:  Scientists and charity field workers are studying nature reserves and other ecosystems to find practical solutions to threats including global warming and expanding human populations.

• *Renewable energy*:  Researchers, often backed by existing fossil fuel companies as well as green organizations, are developing alternative power sources that are sustainable and low in carbon emissions.

• *Pollution*:  Many bodies, usually backed by national governments, have paid for projects to find practical methods of preventing toxic substances entering soil, air, and water systems.

• *Carbon emissions*:  Scientists are looking for ways of "capturing" carbon emitted from power stations and other sources, and storing it so it does not enter the atmosphere.

• *Food production*:  A number of green charities support research into more sustainable farming methods, including the use of organic fertilizers, feeds, and **pesticides**.

## Who pays for research?

A lot of scientific research is highly specialized work, which takes place in laboratories equipped with the latest aids and expert knowledge. Few charities have the money or space to run establishments like this. So the research is done by universities or colleges that have the equipment and the top academic scientists.

Projects at environmental research laboratories are given financial support by charities and by **government agencies**. For example, the Environmental Change Institute at Oxford University is one of the leading green research centres in the world. Its recent projects include helping to plan the United Kingdom's long-term policies on energy and transport. This was partly paid for by government bodies such as UK Energy Research.

## The moral question

*Charities have difficult choices. Many rely on large and regular donations of money from businesses of all kinds. But are these companies genuinely interested in helping the environment, or are they just anxious to be seen as "green"? Should charities accept donations from anyone? Or should they reject those companies who do not follow fair and ethical principles? For example, some non-profit bodies conduct research into new, cleaner and greener fuels. Petrol companies such as BP may help to pay for this research. Such companies have caused widespread environmental damage, through disasters such as oil spills. But their support might make the world less reliant on oil. What choice should the charity make?*

Research into plant growth plays a vital part in encouraging food production in threatened areas of the world.

# The work of Earthwatch

The Earthwatch Institute is an environmental organization that funds projects all over the world. Its central aim is to use research to help protect Earth and its ecosystems. It believes that future decisions about the environment will have to be based on proper scientific study.

## Bringing experts and students together

People are at the core of Earthwatch's research projects. This means not just qualified scientists and experts, but also volunteers and students with little or no experience. The Institute wants to get ordinary people working in field research and education. This will help them understand the environment, and what action is needed to make it sustainable.

Since the charity was founded in 1971, it has sent more than 85,000 volunteers out into the field to work alongside scientists all over the world. The volunteers pay for their adventure, and so contribute funds to the projects. But in return they learn about conservation and the need to take responsibility for the environment. Many go home inspired to work for change in their own communities.

## Where are the projects?

Here is a selection from over 100 Earthwatch research projects worldwide:

- California, USA: tracing plant changes in response to climate change and development
- Mongolia: discovering and documenting the indigenous culture of the **steppes**
- Bahamas: monitoring the health of coral reefs and the impact of climate change
- Borneo: helping scientists assess the effect of global warming and collect data to help with restoring damaged rainforest areas
- Canada: helping to record data from the edge of the Arctic ice to show the effect of rising global temperatures
- Kenya: working with indigenous peoples to build sustainable economies and study interactions between humans and wildlife.

## Volunteer on the ice

"My keen interest in the environment was really awakened during my time working with the charity Earthwatch. In 2006, I was a team member on their Icelandic Glaciers expedition, one of the many expeditions run by Earthwatch that allow volunteers to get directly involved in 'hands-on' environmental research," says Clare Marl.

The Skaftafell region contains the largest glacier in Europe and two vast volcanoes hidden under the ice. One of these had erupted in 1996, causing disastrous floods. Since then, a team of researchers has been making a close study of the area and the impact of the natural disaster. The team had to work under extreme conditions. The weather could change suddenly from sunshine to storms, and the wind chill could lower temperatures within a few minutes.

Some of the volunteers worked on mapping and surveying changes. Some used radar to measure the depth of sand and ice. Others used satellite-positioning systems to record the speed and direction of the glacier's movement. These studies meant the researchers would be able to predict what might happen if another eruption occurred.

The volunteers learned just how sensitive glaciers are to rises in temperature, whether from volcanic eruptions or from changing climates. This makes them important indicators of global warming.

Earthwatch researchers trekked for several miles across sandy wasteland before reaching the Icelandic glacier.

## Researchers at work

Research teams have many ways of operating. Some work in laboratories, some in experimental workshops, and some in live consumer surveys in the street or over the phone. Here are two contrasting research projects in two very different settings.

## In the office...

*"EWG Meat Eater's Guide Spotlights Beef's Outsize Carbon Footprint"*

This headline to a press release in July 2011 by the Environmental Working Group (EWG) announced the publication of the *Meateater's Guide to Climate Change and Health*. It showed just how much our food choices can affect our environment and our health.

The evidence for the guide was gathered by EWG researchers in the organization's offices in Washington DC, USA. The team was led by Kari Hamerschlag, who also wrote the final report. Kari is a senior analyst with EWC in the areas of agriculture and climate change.

The object of the research was to closely study 20 types of food through every step of their production. How much carbon was emitted during the entire food cycle? Using specially designed computer programs, the team was able to calculate these "carbon footprints" – from sowing the seed, through harvesting and processing the crop, to eating the food, and disposing of the waste.

The results showed that eating less meat and cheese is not only healthier but causes lower greenhouse gas emissions. "By eating and wasting less meat, consumers can help limit the environmental damage caused by the huge amounts of fertilizer, fuel, water, and pesticides, not to mention the toxic manure and wastewater, that goes along with producing meat," says Kari.

## ...and in the wild

Peter and Emma Ashton are a husband-and-wife team who share the job of managing a nature reserve at Boolcoomatta in South Australia. This massive reserve was bought by the conservation charity Bush Heritage in 2006. Bush Heritage manages land of special environmental value, and protects its plants, animals, and habitats. "I often refer to ourselves as nature farmers," says Emma, "because we live in much the same way as any farmer, but without the stock or crops."

Boolcoomatta is a strange place to call home. It is surrounded by vast, treeless plains covered in grey saltbush and prickly acacia shrubs. And it is remote. The nearest town, Broken Hill, is over 100 kilometres (70 miles) away. There is no school nearby, so the children get their learning over the radio.

Looking after the reserve is hard work. Peter and Emma fix fences, control predators, root out invasive plants, and generally protect the extraordinary ecosystem. They are helped by Bush Heritage's teams of ecologists and volunteers, who also carry out regular surveys of the animals and plants there. Rare species found at Boolcoomatta include the dusky hopping-mouse and the purplewood wattle tree.

This research is important for two reasons. First, it shows whether Bush Heritage is using the right conservation methods. If numbers of rare animals and plants are increasing, then the methods are clearly working. Secondly, the research can be used to help build up a picture of habitat conservation all over Australia. This is very valuable, because the country is already suffering from the effects of climate change.

Annette Ruzicka and Emma Ignjic from Bush Heritage enjoy a morning bush walk with the local children.

# A VISION FOR THE FUTURE

Environmental action is all about the future. The object of green charities is to protect the Earth's ecosystems and inhabitants from disastrous damage, so that future generations can have safe and healthy lives. But the threat of disaster is growing and changing all the time. Charities and other organizations will have to adapt to cope with this.

## Campaigning together

Local environmental action will need to involve groups covering the whole community. This will make any campaign much more powerful, so that pressure on local and national government, and on businesses, will be stronger. It also means that all sides of an issue will be thoroughly examined. Green organizations in several communities are already getting together in this way.

For example, many cities have very congested road systems. Slow road traffic harms the environment in many ways, including increased air pollution and wasting of fossil fuels. Cleaner and greener transport networks need to be developed. This can only be done efficiently if different pressure groups work together. They include organizations which campaign for:

- car-sharing (so fewer cars are needed)
- cleaner air (controlling emissions)
- road tolls (making drivers pay for using the roads)
- congestion charging (drivers with more polluting vehicles pay more)
- cycle paths (making the use of bicycles more attractive)
- greener public transport (using, for example, electric tram systems).

## Getting more support from industry

Many environmental charities see big business as the main enemy of the environment. Mining, oil-drilling, and manufacturing companies, and industrialized farming methods have certainly caused a great deal of damage. However, large corporations have a huge amount of influence and money, and cannot be ignored. They have to become a major part of the answer instead of the problem.

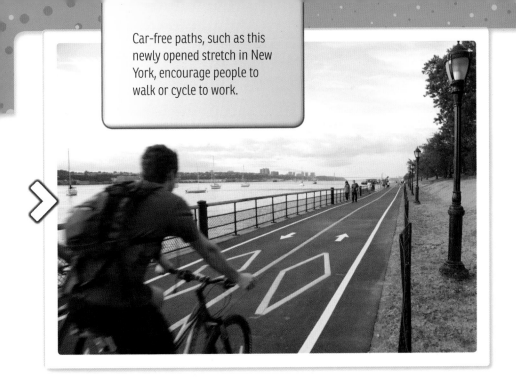

Car-free paths, such as this newly opened stretch in New York, encourage people to walk or cycle to work.

The BlueGreen Alliance is one organization that is trying to bring industry and environmental groups closer together. It believes that conservation issues, such as renewable energy and other practical solutions to global warming, will transform the world economy. The Alliance is building a partnership between environmental organizations and labour unions, aimed at increasing the number of jobs in the new green industries.

## Using new technology

Charities depend on printed and broadcast media to get their message across to the public. But new ways of communicating are being developed all the time. Many organizations already employ methods including online advertising and mobile phone texting.

### Confronting climate change globally

*"No nation can address this challenge on its own. No region can insulate itself from these climate changes. That is why we need to confront climate change within a global framework, one that guarantees the highest level of international cooperation."*

Ban Ki-Moon, Secretary General of the United Nations

# Care and affection: the international Tunza project for children

Children are the future of the environment. A Native American proverb says "We do not inherit the Earth from our ancestors, we borrow it from our children". So it is vital that green organizations send a strong message to young people about the importance of looking after the planet in years to come. One very successful movement is the Tunza project, run by the United Nations Environment Program (UNEP).

## Making young people aware

UNEP launched the new project in 2003. *Tunza* means "to treat with care and affection" in Swahili (an East African language). The concept of the Tunza project was built around "care and affection" for the Earth, and for the people on it.

The aim of Tunza is to get young people engaged with green activities and, especially, in the work done by UNEP itself. This includes becoming aware of environmental threats, learning ways of dealing with these threats, and exchanging views with other young people all over the world. With this background, the next generation of adults should be equipped to take positive action to protect their planet.

The 2011 Tunza Children and Youth Conference in Bandung, Indonesia, brought together young representatives from all over the world.

# Getting together

Tunza is all about taking responsibility for the future. This means joining one of the youth networks run by the organization in many parts of the world, and being active in green campaigns, especially those promoted by UNEP. During 2011, for example, Tunza members took part in many events involved with International Year of the Forests, World Water Day, and the Big Help Environment Campaign.

Here are some of the other activities for Tunza members:

- *The Tunza International Children and Youth Conference on the Environment*

In September 2011, over 1,400 young people came together in Bandung, Indonesia. They met to discuss a range of green topics, such as a new United Nations initiative called "Reshaping Our Future Through a Green Economy and Sustainable Lifestyle". They also discussed more environmentally friendly ways of living.

- *TUNZA Magazine*

This monthly magazine is written "for youth, by youth, about youth". It contains articles about a huge variety of green issues, from rainforests to recycling, as well as blogs and environmental news.

- *The International Children's Painting Competition on the Environment*

This competition is held every year and is open to children aged between 6 and 14 years. Winners are picked for each region of the world, and there are also five global winners.

## What is UNEP?

The United Nations Environment Program runs conservation activities all over the world for the United Nations. It helps less economically developed countries to adopt green policies, promotes environmental research, and organizes major conferences. UNEP's headquarters are in Nairobi, Kenya.

# VOLUNTEERING

Throughout this book, we have met several people who have volunteered to work for environmental charities. We have heard about their adventures, and learned about some of the work they have done. Would you like to be a volunteer? This chapter tells you about the realities of the job, the hundreds of opportunities on offer, and how to find out more.

## Why be a volunteer?

In simple terms, a volunteer is someone who does unpaid work for a charity. Why do people want to do this? Research has shown that there are three main reasons:

1. *To help a cause they believe in.* Someone who feels very strongly about green issues, such as climate change or pollution, will be eager to take practical action. This supports the cause and connects volunteers to it. It also gives people a sense of self-worth and fulfilment.

2. *To meet other people who think the same as them.* Voluntary work brings together people who often have the same ideals. They then share the experience of working together in sometimes testing circumstances. This can create long-lasting friendships.

3. *To learn something new and valuable.* Many environmental charities offer research work, world travel, and other experiences that give people fresh knowledge about the world. Some bodies even give specific training in some tasks.

## What is volunteer work really like?

Charity jobs come in all shapes and sizes. Volunteers may be employed close to home – as administrators in the office, as fundraisers in the street or on the telephone, or as helpers at charity events or rallies. This kind of work is often hard and not very glamorous. It can include simple tasks such as filling envelopes, stacking chairs, or delivering newsletters.

A lot of environmental volunteers may want jobs in the field, either at home or abroad. These involve work which may be seen as much more exciting. It could be helping scientists with their research in remote locations, such as the Amazon rainforest or the Arctic ice fields, or planting trees in Indonesia, or collecting medicinal plants in Kenya.

But fieldwork is not always as exotic as that, and the job may be difficult at times. You may be working in an office or in a city, rather than the great outdoors. Or you may have to cope with bad weather and unfamiliar working conditions. Then there is the chance of homesickness, living in a place that is remote and strange to you. Volunteers have to be resourceful enough to cope with the bad times as well as the good.

## Some quotes about volunteering

"Those who can, do. Those who can do more, volunteer."

Author unknown

"Volunteers are vital to enabling this country to live up to the true promise of its heritage."

Bill Clinton, US president, 1993–2001

"You shouldn't go through life with a catcher's mitt on both hands. You need to be able to throw something back."

Maya Angelou, US writer and poet

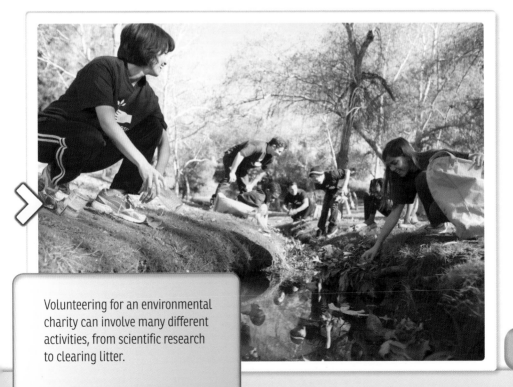

Volunteering for an environmental charity can involve many different activities, from scientific research to clearing litter.

## What do you need to be a volunteer?

Whether you are doing voluntary work at home or in a foreign country, you need certain qualities and experiences to see you through. By being able to cope with widely differing situations, you will be a happier and more effective volunteer.

Charities will also be more likely to give you a job if you can prove that you have the right attitude and abilities. You should:

- be able to work hard and steadily under pressure;
- be able to communicate and get on with a wide variety of people;
- have some experience of working in community projects or with disadvantaged people;
- be good at staying focused.

You may begin by feeling that you can change the world with your efforts, then get disappointed when things do not go exactly to plan. Do not have unrealistic expectations, and keep concentrating on the job in front of you.

If you aim to work overseas, you should also:

- have experience of working in another language. This does not necessarily mean being fluent – just able to make yourself understood. The most widely useful languages (other than English) are French and Spanish;
- have enough skill and experience to give training to others. Again, you do not have to be a qualified expert, but it helps if you have some knowledge of, for example, first aid, simple mechanics, teaching, or IT;
- be able to cope with being far away from home for weeks or even months;
- be happy to live in simple conditions, such as tents or huts, without running water, and with unfamiliar food and manners.

## How much does it cost?

Voluntary work is, of course, unpaid. There are still costs involved for things such as travel, accommodation, and food.

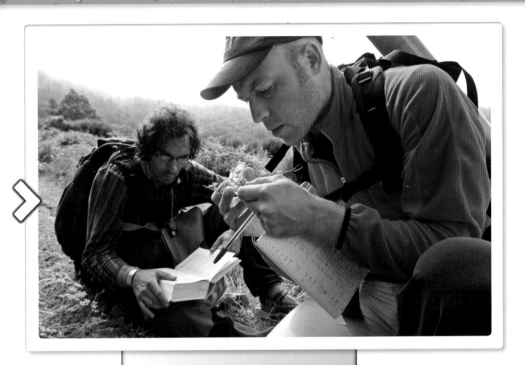

Green volunteers can get to many dramatic places, such as the Pyrenees mountains in France.

Some charities will cover your expenses for you, as they may be included in grants they receive from government and other sources. But others (especially smaller organizations) may expect you to pay for yourself.

If you are volunteering for an environmental charity near your home, these expenses will be very little. But if you are going overseas, charities will almost certainly ask for sums to cover food, travel, and sleeping arrangements. These costs can be as much as £70 a week or more. If you have a qualified skill – for example, in medicine or engineering – you probably will not have to pay.

It pays to do as much research as possible before you apply for a post. On pages 62–63 you will find a list of websites that will give you guidance and ideas about volunteering at home and overseas.

## ⟩ FACTS AND FIGURES

### Climate change: some facts

• Eleven of the last 12 years have been the hottest since 1850, when records began.

• Global temperatures have risen by 0.76°C (1.37°F) in the past 150 years.

• The amount of carbon dioxide in Earth's atmosphere has risen by 35 per cent since 1750 – the start of the industrial age.

• Sea levels have been rising by an average of 3 millimetres (0.118 inches) a year since 1993. This is due not just to melting icecaps, but also to the fact that the oceans are getting warmer and expanding.

• The area covered by sea ice in the Arctic has fallen by an average of 8 per cent since 1978, an area of 1,036,000 square kilometres (400,000 square miles).

• The proportion of carbon dioxide in Earth's atmosphere has increased from about 280 parts per million before the industrial age (c. 1700 BC) to 382 parts per million in 2006. Almost all of the increase is due to human activity.

• During the period from 1900 to 2006, there was an increase in rainfall over North America, Europe, and northern Asia. But rainfall decreased over land between the tropics. At the same time, the Sahel region and southern Africa, as well as parts of southern Asia, became drier.

• There were 27 full-scale storms recorded during the Atlantic hurricane season of 2005. This is more than ever before.

• Since about 1700, the oceans have become more acidic. Scientists believe this is the result of increased carbon dioxide emissions due to human activity. This acidity restricts the growth of corals, shellfish, and other sea creatures.

## Volunteer statistics

*United States*: 63.4 million adults (26 per cent of the population) volunteered to help their community, giving 8.1 billion hours of service (2009 figures).

*United Kingdom*: 29.1 million adults (41 per cent of the population) volunteered to help their community: 42 per cent of these were women, and 38 per cent men (2009 figures).

*Australia*: 5.2 million adults (34 per cent of the population) took part in voluntary work, giving 713 million hours to the community; 36 per cent of these were women, and 32 per cent men (2006 figures).

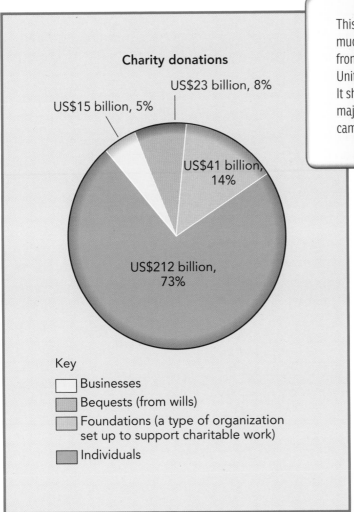

**Charity donations**

US$23 billion, 8%

US$15 billion, 5%

US$41 billion, 14%

US$212 billion, 73%

Key

☐ Businesses
▨ Bequests (from wills)
▨ Foundations (a type of organization set up to support charitable work)
▨ Individuals

This is a pie chart of how much was donated, and from what source, in the United States in 2010. It shows that the vast majority of donations came from individuals.

# GLOSSARY

**accretion** build-up of material such as sand or shingle

**activist** someone who uses strong and direct action to campaign for a cause

**agrofuel** fuel made from crops that are specially grown for the purpose (also known as biofuel)

**archive** place where public records or historical documents are kept

**biodiversity** wide variety of biological forms in an area, such as plants, animals, birds, and insects

**budget** summary of income and expenses over a given period

**carbon** one of the most common elements, which occurs in many forms. It can combine with oxygen (another element) to form carbon dioxide. Carbon is one of the main causes of global warming.

**carbon footprint** calculation of the amount of carbon used or emitted on behalf of a person or organization

**degradation** the ruining of farmland by pollution, or the loss of soil fertility by other causes

**economy** managing of money and other resources of a country or business

**ecosystem** community of plants and animals, together with their environment

**emission** giving off of exhaust gases or other materials

**erosion** wearing away of soil or rock by the wind, the sea, or other forces

**ethical** fitting in with a code of morals or behaviour

**food sovereignty** the right of people to a supply of healthy food produced by clean and sustainable methods

**fossil fuel** fuel, such as coal or petroleum, that was created by the decay of ancient vegetation or animals

**global warming** rise in the temperature of the atmosphere, caused mainly by climate change

**government agency** organization set up by a national government to perform a specific activity

**greenhouse gas** gas such as carbon dioxide which builds up in Earth's atmosphere, absorbing heat from the Sun and thus causing a rise in temperature. Greenhouse gases are a major cause of climate change.

**habitat** type of environment where an animal, plant, or other organism lives

**icecap** covering of snow and ice (as, for example, at the North and South Poles)

**indigenous** native, or living naturally in an area

**intern** person employed to learn a business or skill, often without pay

**less economically developed country** one of the poorer countries of the world, including the countries of Africa, Asia (except for Japan), Latin America, and the Caribbean

**lobby** conduct activities aimed at influencing public officials

**monitor** watch and study carefully, and keep records of something

**non-profit organization** a body which does not distribute its surplus income or funds, but uses them to finance its projects

**nuclear energy** energy made by splitting the nucleus (central part of an atom) of a uranium atom

**pesticide** chemical which is sprayed on ground to destroy animal and insect pests which harm crops

**photo-voltaic cell** cell which converts the rays of the Sun directly into electricity

**pollution** the spoiling or poisoning of air, water, or soil with harmful substances

**press release** announcement of an event or other news given to the media (newspapers, TV, and radio)

**radioactive** giving out radiation in the form of electronic particles from uranium and other unstable elements, or from a nuclear reaction

**solar energy** system that uses the energy of the Sun to produce heat or electricity

**steppe** large, flat area of land with grass and very few trees, found in eastern Europe and Asia

**sustainable energy** energy source that will not run out, and can be renewed

**turbine** machine that is turned by flowing energy such as wind or water, and converts it into electricity

**wetland** lowland area, such as a marsh or swamp, which is permanently wet

# ⟫ FIND OUT MORE

Here are some suggestions for discovering more information about environmental charities and the causes that they support. You will find much more information online, or at your local library or bookshop.

## Books

*Earth-friendly Energy* (Saving Our Living Earth), Ron Fridell (Lerner, 2010)

*Energy Resources* (Maps of the Environmental World), Jack and Meg Gillett (Wayland, 2010)

*Heroes of the Environment: True Stories of People Who Are Helping to Protect Our Planet*, Harriet Rohmer (Chronicle Books, 2009)

*Saving Energy* (Green Kids), Neil Morris (Quarto, 2009)

*Solar Power* (Energy for Today), Tea Benduhn (Gareth Stevens, 2008)

## Websites

**www.charity-volunteer.com/why-do-people-volunteer.html**
Interesting material on why people volunteer and what they do.

**www.childrenoftheearth.org/index.htm**
A fun-filled environmental education site.

**www.ecokids.ca**
Games, stories, pictures, and facts about the environment.

**www.energysavingtrust.org.uk/Easy-ways-to-stop-wasting-energy**
Tips on simple ways to save energy at home.

**www.green-energysaving.com**
Advice on everything from wind turbines to greener homes.

**www.kidsforsavingearth.org**
A wide range of resources and links for teachers and parents.

**planetgreen.discovery.com › Work & Connect**
Help and advice with choosing a charity to donate to.

*Some major green organizations:*
Friends of the Earth: **www.foei.org**
Greenpeace: **www.greenpeace.org/international**
The Rainforest Alliance: **www.rainforest-alliance.org/work/climate**
WWF: **www.wwf.org.uk/oneplanet**

For more information on protests and breaking the law, see:
**www.edo.org.au/edonsw/site/factsh/fs10_7.php**

For more figures about charity spending, look on: **www.charitynavigator.org**

To find out more about the pros and cons of celebrities' involvement with charities, look on:
**www.forbes.com/2010/06/30/oprah-jolie-pitt-letterman-philanthropy-personal-finance-celebrity-charities.html** or **www.bbc.co.uk/news/magazine-12357524**

Find out more about Tunza projects on the UNEP website:
**www.unep.org/tunza/children/events**

Websites with information about volunteering at home and overseas:
**www.do-it.org.uk**

A straightforward guide to volunteering, backed by the charity YouthNet:
**money.howstuffworks.com/economics/volunteer/information/volunteer-vacations.htm**

An introduction to the costs of volunteering and other issues:
**www.goabroad.com/volunteer-abroad/search/united-states/volunteer-abroad-1**

A directory of volunteer jobs available overseas, with opportunities for environmental work in more than 50 countries: **www.earthwatch.org/europe**

A wide range of voluntary jobs in developing countries:
**www.vso.org.uk/volunteer-placements**

## DVDs

*An Inconvenient Truth*, featuring Al Gore (2008)
This film formed an important part of Gore's campaign to publicize the dangers of global warming.

*The Eleventh Hour*, starring Leonardo di Caprio (2008)
This film documents the perils facing many of the planet's life systems.

*The Truth about Climate Change*, featuring Sir David Attenborough (2008)
The famous naturalist travels the world to find shocking evidence of climate change.

# INDEX